About *The M[*]*

M000187128

It is good to wake and realize that Molly is paying attention, has paid so much attention, and we are not lost. What a fine poet! She is the real thing!

— *Lucille Clifton*

With unflinching honesty, kind humor, and vivid detail, Molly Fisk convinces us 'There's a loveliness to every ruined thing.' *The More Difficult Beauty* is a brave and generous book.

— *Ellen Bass*

Whether writing of the way light falls on Paris rooftops, family remembrances and betrayals, the fragility of intimacy, or the physicality and metaphysics of blood, Molly Fisk does not hold back. Unblinking, she sets down dramatically whatever turns up in her poet-mirror. Fisk's poems twinkle with the dark, nuanced subtlety of painted miniatures; they speak from the heart and gut. Devils and angels dwell in her details.

— *Al Young*

About Molly Fisk's debut collection, *Listening to Winter* (Heyday Press, 1999):

"...[an] intellectually self-aware, bold and brilliant re/consideration of the culturally paradigmatic problem of incest. In lacunae and ellipses as artful as the poems themselves, she shows to the mind the heart's wounds and forces it to make of them an answer. Complex, memorable, *Listening to Winter* makes vivid the real and dangerous work of what is called, contemptuously, 'confessionalism,' meditating, from its most intimate perspective, on the nature and costs of 'The Old Order.'"

— *Linda McCarriston*

Hip Pocket Press Mission Statement

It is our belief that the arts are the embodiment of the soul of a culture, that the promotion of writers and artists is essential if our current culture, with its emphasis on television and provocative outcomes, is to have a chance to develop that inner voice and ear that express and listen to beauty. Toward that end, Hip Pocket Press will continue to search out and discover poets and writers whose voices can give us a clearer understanding of ourselves and of the culture which defines us.

Other Books from Hip Pocket Press

You Notice the Body; Gail Rudd Entrekin (poetry)

Terrain; Dan Bellm, Molly Fisk, Forrest Hamer (poetry)

A Common Ancestor; Marilee Richards (poetry)

Sierra Songs & Descants: Poetry & Prose of the Sierra

Truth Be Told; Tom Farber (epigrams)

Songs for a Teenage Nomad; Kim Culbertson (young adult fiction)

Yuba Flows; Kirsten Casey, Gary Cooke, Cheryl Dumesnil, Judy Halebsky, Iven Lourie & Scott Young (poetry)

Web Publications

Canary, a Literary Journal of the Environmental Crisis; www.hippocketpress.com/canary.cfm

Sisyphus, Essays on Language, Culture & the Arts; www.hippocketpress.com/sisyphus.cfm

The More Difficult Beauty

Also by Molly Fisk

<u>Poems</u>

Listening to Winter
Terrain (with Forrest Hamer and Dan Bellm)
Salt Water Poems

<u>Radio Commentary (CDs)</u>

Blow-Drying a Chicken
Using Your Turn Signal Promotes World Peace

The More Difficult Beauty

Molly Fiske
~~Molly Fiske~~

*with great love
and admiration
for Molly and
Saun terre
Nevada City
xox Molly*

HPP
HIP POCKET PRESS

Orinda, CA
2010

Published by Hip Pocket Press
5 Del Mar Court
Orinda, CA 94563
www.hippocketpress.com

This edition was produced for on-demand distribution by
lightningsource.com for Hip Pocket Press.

Typesetting: Wordsworth (wordsworthofmarin.com)
Cover design: Brook Design Group (brookdesign.com)

Author photo: Alan Pomatto
Proofreading: Judy Crowe

Cover photo by Steve Solinsky (solinskyphoto.com)

Printed in the United States of America.

ISBN 10: 0917658-36-1
ISBN 13: 978-0-917658-36-5

Acknowledgements

88: Journal of Contemporary American Poetry: "Prayer for Joe's Taco Lounge, Mill Valley"

American Literary Review: "Theology"

ARTWORKS: "Little Songs for Antoinette"

Beatitude: "Poem for the Rest of Us"

The Coe Review: "Women at Forty"

Convergence (on-line): "The Way a Daughter Would Know Her," "Winter Sun"

Cortland Review (on-line): "In the Fifth Year of Our War"

Dogwood: "Washington Square—New York, 1941"

Haight Ashbury Literary Journal: "Daughters"

The Healing Woman: "Daughters," "Eulogy for Junior Mints"

MARGIE Review: "Unwrapping the Last French Menstrual Napkin," "Not All Who Wander Are Lost"

Michigan Quarterly Review: "The Color of Apricots," "The October Garden"

The New College Review: "Poem for the Rest of Us"

Nimrod: "The Seine"

Poetry Daily (on-line): "The October Garden" (reprinted from *Michigan Quarterly Review*)

poetrymagazine.com (on-line): "Love Songs," "Eulogy for Junior Mints," "Tiles on a Temple Wall at Luangphrabang"

River Oak Review: "Forced Narcissus" (under the title "Forsythia"), "Windfall"

Schuylkill Valley Journal: "Travel," "I Think of Them"

Stand: "Truckee River," "What to Wear"

Talking River: "American Riddle"

The Union: "Little Songs for Antoinette"

Willow Springs: "Double Solitaire"

Zone 3: "Missing him, suddenly," "Kindness"

"First Winter," and "Kindling" appeared in the collaborative chapbook *Terrain*, by Dan Bellm, Molly Fisk, and Forrest Hamer (Hip Pocket Press, 1998). "Washington Square—New York, 1941" received the Dogwood Prize in 2007 was nominated for a 2007 Pushcart Prize. "Rowing, November" appeared in the anthology *Cloud View Poets: Master Classes with David St. John,* and on the Radcliffe College Crew's 30th anniversary webpage. "Little Songs for Antoinette" received the Robinson Jeffers Tor House Prize in Poetry in 2005. "Kindness" appeared in the PBS documentary "The Loss of Nameless Things," directed by Bill Rose, 2005. "Doe Bay in September" appeared in the California Poets in the Schools Anthology: *Moon Won't Leave Me Alone.* "Daughters" was included in *Writing Our Way Out of the Dark* (Queen of Swords Press, 1995), and *This Far Together* (*Haight Ashbury Literary Journal* Anthology, 1995).

My love and thanks to Dan Bellm & Forrest Hamer, Dorianne Laux, Marilyn Kriegel, Margot Silk Forrest, Sharon Olds, Robert Hass, Galway Kinnell, Lucille Clifton, Oakley Hall III, Julia Kelliher & Joanna Robinson, Maxima Kahn, Fred Marchant, Molly Peacock, Kim Addonizio, Joyce Jenkins, Thekla Clemens, Judie Rae, Nancy Burns Trice & Laura Pendell, Joe Millar, Geri Digiorno & Judy Stedman, Paula Elliott, Tim Underwood, Bill Lee, Bill Larsen, Susan Robinson, Ellen Bass & Laura Davis, Carl & Marie Dern, Gail & Charles Entrekin, Steve Solinsky, Alan Pomatto, Justin Bailey, and the Are-We-Meeting-This-Friday-Afternoon? Gang: Jacquie Bellon, Kate Dwyer, Liz Collins, Sandra Rockman, Valerie Kack-Brice, Jeff Kane & Ronnie Paul.

CONTENTS

Fire

Color

Anger

Light

Time

for my mother

Daybreak

Dark still, and cold—the cats have me pinned
    under too few covers. What was I dreaming? Something
with uneasiness I can still taste. A hawk in one of my pines
    is piercing the wind over and over with his call.
Except there is no wind. Too bad for the poem,
    but once you start lying for beauty, it's over.
Dale says those are young Red-tails who call like that, unending.
    I've decided to believe him: he's the sort who squats
to smell unfamiliar scat and poke it with a stick to see
    what the shitter was eating. I know this is a hawk.
But how do I know it? Years trailing my grandmother
    as she explained, then short bursts of observation.
Even when I learned that Red-tails claim the tops
    of telephone poles while the Red-shouldered (*buteo lineatus*)
prefer the swinging wire, I still couldn't tell them apart.
    And I may have reversed the preferences. At what point
in a life does it matter that you can tell one hawk from another?
    When Joanna sat by a picture window overlooking
Lake Michigan with her demented mother and wanted
    to point out a seagull, its name eluded her menopausal brain.
But her mother said—with kindness, perhaps recognizing
    that stunned look or slipping back to a time when Joanna
pointed at everything—"Let's call it a *bird*." Maybe we don't
    take any distinctions into the grave. I've lost the streets
in Cambridge even though for years I walked and drove them,
    rolled them on my tongue. And what are years?

I think of an oval, a quarter-mile high school track, with winter
        and summer the longer sides. Here it is September,
early for this kind of cold, and we're about to swoop
        through fall, passing those ever-trumpeted social holidays —
until it's as dark as it gets, the gods arraying themselves
        on the bleachers in pea-coats and plaid mufflers
like college kids in the fifties, cheering as we take the bend,
        panting under the weight of our little, incandescent lives,
naming the birds and flowers, naming our children or cats or cars,
        mountain peaks and heretofore undiscovered
star clusters, establishing facts to surround us as protection
        against the void. Trying to avoid all intimation of *the* void.
Words are still a comfort, even as age removes them
        from our grasp. Daybreak, for instance. How did *breaking*
enter someone's mind when light crested the highest hill,
        flooding the world with yellow? I like to think it was a woman
at her baking, one who glanced up as that gold lit the dust of flour,
        the china bowl, who watched the sun's yolk spreading out
across the hill, unbroken—daylight pouring now into the jagged
        shell, halved in her open palm.

Blood

Unwrapping the Last French Menstrual Napkin

It has a slim silhouette and little wings
that wrap around the crotch. The pad
is quilted into diamonds, the paper backing
easy to peel off and the color
a faded rosy-peach, as elegant as any
feminine so-called hygiene product
I have ever seen. The last of fourteen
serviettes I bought in a pharmacy in Paris
a month ago, hoping to find what I needed
and not have to use my high-school French
to describe. I am almost 50. This is the 457th
period I've entertained, excluding
the one I missed before the abortion in April,
1984. That child would turn 20 next November,
and how much I wish I had kept it now
that I have no others, all those dropped eggs
flushed with their hopeful rejuvenating
uterine linings and only a few left
to make the passage, tiny raisins now,
the once-plump grapes that swelled inside
my mother as she swam in her mother's womb
and all for nothing, the last of a daughterless,
motherless woman, one who is unmarried
and today feeling horribly sorry for herself, but
who recently has been to France.

Women at Forty

Women at forty
stand in supermarkets listening
for the voices of children
they never had.

Behind them doors close softly.
They walk steadily forward
into the next day and each successive week
as if they don't notice.

Men turn less often to watch them pass,
although the younger ones, still almost boys,
narrow their gazes, noticing something
and wondering if it's valuable.

They stand in front of mirrors
but not to draw the familiar picture
with lipstick and shadow.
They look at themselves. They are used to
the silent bell of the telephone.

It is their mothers' hands now
folded in their own spacious laps.
The tiny diamond lines
patiently etched into the skin,

and the skin beginning to loosen its hold
on the muscles. As if the spaces
between things were widening
inside their bodies, making room

for something entirely new.

after Donald Justice

Little Songs for Antoinette

I.

While my mother is dying I pursue a new man, leave
messages arranging dinner, asking about his book.

Standing behind her, hand on her back, a washcloth ready
as she throws up what's left inside, I think of his long arms

winding my waist, the blue eyes closed in pleasure. I am never
going to die, and not like this:

an eight-months-gone pregnancy of tumors, morphine
every 20 minutes under the tongue. Her cancer makes me want

to have a baby quick, not to replace her but to prove that somewhere
life is winning. This man doesn't know what he's in for,

big hand on the small of my back as we enter the restaurant,
his apartment — he hasn't seen her mouth gape in sleep,

the bones of her hands outlined in parchment, he doesn't understand
the honor: that our hips cupped together hold a single ray of light,

that my tongue against his throat spells her name.

II.

The tears we cry rinse our big hearts clean,
and our mother—past the wail-and-shudder
stage, losing everything—throws up
the two bites of scrambled egg she had for breakfast
and the half glass of water, fills the sink over
with waves from an inner river, the earth
now calling her home. She says she's not
afraid of dying, just the pain and leaving us,
her quartet of old children. Who will take care
of her in heaven? Whose lips will she read there?

III.

At times she dozes, one knee cocked
and her hands lightly holding the bed rails.
If you lean against the door's white jamb
and watch her, love pouring out of your cracked heart
and spilling into the lives around you, she's just
as likely to smile as groan, open her eyes and whisper
beautiful, spinning into the arms of the plum tree
out her window, taking a bow. She asks us
what time the wind gets up in the morning,
hums in her sleep, drums her toothbrush
against the side of the spitting bowl before
we can empty it, happy, laughing at us.

IV.

Now every dream is of my mother
carrying the years she'll never have, her hair
grown in and whiter, approaching rooms
she'll never enter now, and then leaving them
to stroll down avenues she'll never see
because she is almost finished with us
and lies asleep after another dose of morphine
and some chipped ice. I look twice
to make sure she's breathing and the quick
pulse in her throat has not stopped.
I sit beside her crying. The room's temperature
has dropped: she is no longer always cold,
she who will be so cold soon, awake now, briefly,
looking out the window at a new moon.

V.

Helping her die may be better than watching her age and falter,
but we'll never know, sponging her back, filling syringes.

Her eyelids open like hinges on the door to the other world, whorl
of new hair behind her head, skin pearled with a luminous sweat,

stretched over cheek bone and jaw line, beginning death's
paring away of flesh. This is a test — how strong are your children?

Who loves you best? Will you come back to us all in our dreams,
hawk on a fence post, rush of clear water? Two sons, two daughters,

dozing, talking, laundering sheets, wiping the counters,
waiting to hear one more breath.

What's Left

The walker, though she wouldn't use it.
The commode. Syringes in a pewter bowl
arrayed around the morphine bottle like petals.
In the freezer: lemon popsicles, C-Statin, the ice
we smashed that she didn't eat.
On the counter: the rolling pin for smashing.
Clean sheets folded on closet shelves.
Fading flowers in a blue vase, their hundred
predecessors composting in the yard.
The white blouse I ironed for her when we both
knew she wouldn't wear street clothes again.
Photographs of her with hair.
The boarding pass from Phoenix
where the clinic couldn't help her. The thriller
she read on the flight home—a month ago:
she could still read. Two pairs of glasses.
Mail from people we've never met.
Thick books on every surface dispensing cures,
hope, advice on grieving. Unopened boxes of Kleenex.
The kitchen clock's black hands and steady ticking.
The four-wheeled plastic hospital table
and its matching bed. The walker.

Irony

The day she dies my period arrives: slick,
dark, serene, entitled, and I stare at clots
gleaming on the toilet paper somehow entire,
self-contained, American as Jell-o
with no sign of the unfertilized egg, the apparition,
one of my last, lost daughters,
this familiar rosy mess perhaps a sympathetic
message from my uterus, a greeting card,
reminding me of how I once came out between her legs
and met the world and it was good, even though her ovaries —
those little pockets filled with tapioca, my motherland
since she was born — are what finally killed her.

The History of Men

There's a kind of relief in letting the dandelions grow,
letting them bloom egg-yolk yellow and halo their seeds
until the wind carries them everywhere. There is some
inexplicable joy in giving up, in admitting it doesn't matter,
in smiling at each serrated leaf, and sending good will
to the stubborn taproots you once troweled up with a grunt,
folding them all in a plastic bag to take to the dump
where they couldn't survive, where they'd be crushed
into airless cubes with styrofoam cups and torn
lampshades, old sofas whose stuffing is history, mill ends
from somebody's dad teaching his son to build—what?
a birdhouse. There's a secret delight in relinquishing
your will to fight the inevitable.

Though the boy watching his dad is too young to know it.
He has that stubborn, boy-like look in his eyes, the perfect
mix of boredom and disdain for experience, still laced
a little with awe at the power of fathers, of his own father,
man of familiar smells and favorite blue sweater, even after
divorce, even clearly a failure at something, at staying
in the same house with his mom and not yelling, and although
not a failure with hammer and nails, he's failing again
at connecting: showing the boy instead of letting him try it,
using a voice he should leave at work, not looking up
to see the gathering clouds of disappointment darken
his son's eyes. What the boy is learning is isolation in company,
what his mother left his father for in the first place, and even
the lingering scent of cut pine boards doesn't make up
for the hollowness in his stomach later, when he glances out
at that forlorn carpentry project tacked to the fence—
empty, of course.

It will be years before he can look at a yard without seeing
what needs to be mowed and wondering where to hide.
And it's useless to predict the future. But let's wish for him
that someday, when he's reached middle-age and learned
to admit his own failures, maybe even begun to forgive
his father, something inside him will loosen, will gradually
unknot itself and cause him to lie back on the grass,
arms outstretched, trowel forgotten, and watch contrails
divide the sky, and feel his heart's steady kick, and listen
to the sound of dandelions growing.

American Riddle

When you can't figure out how to stop
the war in Iraq, much less how to make
enough money to pay your mortgage,
moving the hundred and eighty dollars
from savings back into your checking
account as if that will help—when it's
all you can do to acknowledge the actual
world and not lose yourself half the afternoon
in *People Magazine* where the movie stars
twirl like frosted cakes in a glass case
at the old Lady Baltimore bakery
on Throckmorton, before your hometown
became so chic none of the kids
from your high school could afford
to live there—when you're so tired
of reinventing yourself you want to lie down
on the road, right on the double yellow line
in front of your driveway, exactly where
two of your cats have been killed and wait
for someone to run you over but with your luck
you'd probably just lose an arm, no doubt
the right one, so you'd have to relearn
holding the pencil against the page
at the proper angle, and your sweater's
sleeves would need to be hemmed
to cover the stump and then you'd really
have something to complain about
as well as something in common with soldiers
back from the Middle East
who left a precious part of themselves behind,
which is where this poem begins and ends:
How the hell are we going to stop the cavalier
waste? How are we going to *apologize*?

The Way a Daughter Would Know Her

Less nurse than wry smile across an easel and,
  "If you're so hungry, *you* make dinner."
Early morning emptier of dish drainers.

Less hiker than salt swimmer, head resolutely above water.
About equal mother and daughter, rarely disobedient as either.
Younger sister. Wicked tennis partner.

Driver of station wagons, stitcher of tiny smocked dresses, knitter
  of reindeer sweaters.
Finder of mittens, repairer of wrenched zippers.

Less gullible than you would at first glance guess.
Reader, when stressed, of Margery Allingham, Robert Frost,
  The New Yorker.

Adlai Stevenson admirer. Staunch arguer for human rights
  but not a public speaker.
Nettler of windbags. Planned Parenthood donor.

Less gin & tonic than Earl Grey, more Yardley's English Lavender
  than Oil of Olay.
Follower of recipes exactly, flour-sifter.

Minister's child, eventual attendant at church but "I only go
  to sing in the choir."
More laugher than joke-teller. Practiced eye-roller.

Quick observer of human emotion, noter of an infinite variety of color.
Unshakeable Vermont-lover, but hold the maple sugar.
Happy wife and then less so of a philanderer as long as she could stand it,
  and lonely after.

At the piano with the same Bach over and over.
More listener than talker but in time ears failed her. Learner
of American Sign.

Ovarian cancer non-survivor.
More alive in mind than a handful of chalk under marble
next to her parents in Saxonville.

Forced Narcissus

An orange leaf was laid on every finger bowl
and the plates were twelve moons orbiting
the candelabra. What you remember about wealth
will come back to you: initials etched
into the silver handle of each serving spoon,
the way steam rises from an uncapped tureen.
Decanting the wine. Run your thumb
along this polished chair, mahogany or fruit-
wood, it won't splinter. The cream-colored
place cards, little sentinels, their dark ink
just dry—swooping A of Antoinette,
voluptuous S of Schuyler. The way what we name
belongs to us, unexpected and tenacious.
A little Brahms floating down from somewhere
in the house, and the stiff forsythia in its cut-
glass cage. Forced narcissus on the mantel.
The carrots for the soup—it is deep winter—
peeled by hand. Turmeric ground in a mortar
and pestle. Linen napkins pulled, near-frozen,
from the cellar line and ironed in relative silence.
And if anyone spoke: the lace
veil of conversation. You were young,
you wanted burlap, loud noise, truth.
Now you have discovered there is no such thing
as truth, and the story of a life is always complicated.
Before you draw the drapes on that snow-
covered drive, light the tapers, watch their brief fire
gild your reflection in the window. This used to be
your home. Look tenderly at everything you hate
to admit: you were born into a house
where an orange leaf was laid on every finger bowl.

Water

Truckee River

Under the blue surface you know it's there, miles of water
      already composed into a river,
coiled around itself inside the deepest lake you know.

And how nonchalantly it spills out of that gate
      beneath the Fanny Bridge,
dropping only 15 feet or so, and begins a docile run

past the lumberyard, meandering through hummocks
      of marshy yellow-green, giving willows
all they need to drink, succoring the Jeffrey pines.

It isn't random, the conspiracy of these ten thousand drops
      gliding in formation past the River Ranch
breaking into white over granite, and ten thousand,

and ten thousand more. The river is stored intact, entire,
      its glittered facets jostling
just below the downed water skiers, half a white styrofoam

cooler top, the sleek diesel-spewing cigarette boats,
      Least Terns wheeling and screaming.
Under the satellites sending back clear photographs of Jupiter

and daylight's invisible long-exploded stars.
      Beneath the vaulted sky reflecting color like a mirror.
Even a shallow dive will take you there.

Rowing, November

The way the body wants to pull its own weight,
    hands curled around the shaft of the oar, drawing it clean

through bitter water as blood rushes out the doors
    of your capable heart and cold air billows into both lungs,

the release a kind of violence, oar's brief rest
    as it's feathered, skimming on air and then the quick

turn, the catch, and it grips its width of river again,
    the body in love with use, flat back muscles tight over

shoulder blades, all the bones of the wrist steady, your arms
    pulling hard and straight, fingers curved loose but ready

to grip if the oar hits a pocket of air or a branch,
    submerged, if it scoops a rat's sodden carcass up to the surface

as you pass. You unclench your teeth but set the jaw
    in concentration. The plates of kneecap slide across their ends

of bone as the big thigh muscles contract, relax,
    begin to shake with joy, doing their work. Frost glazes

the drooping willows. Black-crowned herons
    rustle on their secret branches, ready for sleep while your eyes

search now for the first flare of light to smooth
    the curves of the undersides of bridges, sheen of sweat

across your brow, the body's prayer, and steam
    escaping in puffs from your parted lips, hips

balanced an inch over water, the narrow boat
    surging and gliding into another winter.

The Seine

Every day Paris opens its shutters
to sunlight I dream of Vientiane
and the tin ceilings of the Ha Ha Ha
Cigarette Factory we slept beneath.
Hens pecked in the dooryard
of the Ministry building as we passed,
the French long gone — I pressed
the front of my dress to trap sweat
trickling between my breasts,
the heat like a body over my body
slowly shifting its weight,
the Mekong sluggish and brown,
unlike the Seine, the thatched roofs all
that each house was made of,
with corner posts and sometimes a woven mat
over the dirt, each roof crowned with a TV aerial
catching the signal from Bangkok, each
front stoop a little market for things
we never wanted: soap, large white underpants
from Thailand, colorful junk.
When the sun hits the first slate rooftops of Paris
and makes them shine, it is 3 a.m. in Vientiane.
Bicycles lie beside the roads. Chickens
roost in canopied trees. I will stay here
only a short time and never,
I will never be the same.

Doe Bay in September

Clouds low over the whale-backed islands, tide halfway in
      and the choreography of morning begins again:
a kingfisher glides and swoops—harsh *kikkireeki*—to his perch
      on a cedar limb, a seal's head splits the glassy water,
vee of his wake opening wide behind him. A heron lifts
      her brocade wings and flaps—enormous and slow—
from one side of the bay's mouth to the other, rustles and settles
      on a rock, alert and still. Kelp sways and dips and sways.
A second or two of silence and then below it the ear finds
      what the eye cannot: old tune of salt water when a light-fingered
wind has riffled the channel—laps and gurgles interlocking and breaking apart
      without a shore to magnify or interrupt them, a sound like blood
rushing through veins, like love loosed from a tight heart plunging
      back into the world, entering everything—Heron's indivisible
breath, Seal's liquid eye, that white patch on Kingfisher's pumping wing,
      everything that will miss us only in passing when we're gone.

Not All Who Wander Are Lost

He's just wondering where he might have left
a balpeen hammer, a metal rake. Or what that wire
is doing, unattached from the side of the house.
Perhaps pondering the chimney's slant, how best
to pull it safely down: coaxed with a friend's pickup
and rope, or malleted, stone by crumbling
stone? At 58, he's recognizable, fully himself. The palpable
world recedes; plans, perspectives, drawings, blueprints
float through his head—quick decisions, reversals,
recalibrations. He taps one long finger on the table,
or lights a cigarette, his mind at work. Not like a factory,
the worn machinery clanging in timed bursts,
foreman swearing under his breath as he squints
from the glass room overhead. Nor like the farmer
who eases his plow around the last turn in the upper field,
his rows even, his harrow turning up again and again
the black earth. No, this man thinks like a fisherman:
he casts his gill net wide, hauling in the glistening, silvery
quickness he knows is there, somewhere, multitudinous,
along with unlooked-for surprises: tin cans, kelp, a horseshoe
crab shell, flotsam and jetsam of the shifting sea,
and saves it, tucked away in his brain for later use.
Each idea will be polished a little over the weeks, stored
in a dry place, accessible to him when he needs it, when
he's walking around one day in the yard, for instance,
considering how to pull the chimney down, thinking of
where he might have left that damned balpeen hammer
and the neighbor's blue-handled metal rake.

Sunset, Stinson

Especially the way thin layers of water
            slide up the sand and take on the color
of endings — silver or pewter, never
            ocean blue — and then recede into just
a little spent foam or a half-hearted
            undertow according to the tide and
then again slide up, scattering the quick
            feet of godwits and willets, their curved bills
plunging as the water slips down, toward
            itself, easily, and is taken in.

On Sleepless Nights

they come back to you — moments of revelation
clear as that sound on Arey's Pond when a little wind,
an incoming tide, jostles the rigging so that it rings
against the mast and the chorus of twenty or so
small boats sings together until the planet turns
another inch and the wind dies into echoes and stillness.

Once, astride a row of strawberry plants
at some U-Pick farm outside Chicago, I found my body
was hungry to repeat a motion until my muscles
were so sore they forgot themselves, at last
entirely animal. Decades later I feel the heat,
the red stain my hands held, the companionship
of working in silence, shining abundance of berries.

Another straddle, exploring a different hunger
in a hotel room in Baltimore, when I knew
the man was wrong and the situation was hopeless,
that I'd abort the child we made if we made one,
and we did. Sunlight hitting the wall over the headboard
in a bittersweet parallelogram, shape of a window open
onto nothing, an empty mirror.

Cache Creek

Everything I've lost is here in the eddies,
the face I had when I was young reflecting
in still water, the voices of my lovers
audible in ripples. This mud on the bank
is the work I didn't love and that arching
branch the enterprise that saved me. Wet stones
beneath my feet are the lullabies I've sung
to other people's children. The deepest pool
is where I drowned my own.

Sugar

Eulogy for Junior Mints

When I was in high school
my mother would buy them at 7-Eleven
to eat by herself in the car, departing
from some diet, but she'd never hide the boxes—
just toss them onto the back seat's floor
and forget, then be embarrassed when
we saw them and change the subject.

They taste best in front of flickering movie screens,
laid on a willing boyfriend's tongue, or eaten
by halves in bed the day before your period.
White box with its cheerful letters, green
and minty, unchanged from the '50s.
The faintly plastic texture.

When I think of my extra weight:
the soft flesh around my ribs and the bolster
resting on my hips, it's not the doctor's office
picture: anonymous woman of normal size
outlined with yellow lumps. And it isn't the slippery
fat lodged under the skin, so hard to pull off
when you're boning a chicken. I look at myself
in the mirror—larger than most, but not unlovely—
and imagine a layer of Junior Mints
arranged over my muscles, those dark
brown spheres with their creamy centers—
molecules of pleasure.

Candy Bar Tutorial

What he leaves on the bed or slips into her pocket
after the carwash, during the Saturday hike:
Baby Ruth, Mounds, Big Hunk, Milky Way, Bit-O-Honey.

What he whispers: *you made me do it; don't pretend
you don't like it — if you tell, I'll hurt your mother.*
What he leaves on the bed or slips into her pocket

she eats right then or sneaks into a shoebox
at the top of the closet. Her mother won't like it.
Mounds, Big Hunk, Milky Way, Baby Ruth, Bit-O-Honey.

When the man in the next town murders his wife
with a nail gun, she thinks of ten-pennies scattered among
what he leaves on the bed or slips into her pocket.

Setting the table for dinner, knife blades face inward.
The aluminum taste in her mouth is almost erased by
Milky Way, Baby Ruth, Big Hunk, Mounds, Bit-O-Honey

but not completely, still the hint of brine, to remind
her of home and family, sickening harmony:
what he left on the bed and slipped into her pocket:
Big Hunk, Milky Way, Baby Ruth, Mounds, Bit-O-Honey.

Windfall

Deer have eaten the pear's branches at the tips, leaf and stem,
devoured the windfalls, and taken delicate bites from what
they could reach above their heads—the indentations
more rabbit than whitetail, the wounds bound over a little,
no longer bleeding juice.

As I twist the fruit from its birthplace,
what once was a blossom's sunny interior, I start to sing
a Scottish air my mother taught us in childhood, a man overhearing
a woman singing a prayer to her lover, gone to sea, that his keel
may row well, that his blue bonnet stay on his head.
I love its layered nature: someone telling someone else's story,
even though it becomes his own in the telling, how we absorb
the world around us, and pass it on. And the woman, singing
her worry into something almost holy, something a stranger
walking through the gate into town will remember.
Since I was young, listening to my mother's alto harmonize
with the slosh of soapy water in the kitchen sink, I've hoped
the sailor came back to her, I've hoped it hard, and even though
with age I know more about the futility of hope
and the unlikeliness of happy endings, whenever I sing the song
it feels like there might be a chance he did.

Each pear is paired,
I see: they grow on doubled stems. When one is plucked
the other follows. Rather than stay aloft alone it tumbles down.
The multitude of pears is my own windfall, tree that I pruned
in March and then ignored, giving and giving its sweetness
into my hands, the baskets filling and overflowing, the flesh crisp,
white, the skin some unnameable color of green. Green-
when-everything-else-is-turning-gold-and-crimson, last-true-
green-of-a-difficult-summer, green-for-the-reunion-of-every-sailor-
with-every-bonnie-lass, green-of-the-unpredictably-generous-world.

Fire

Prayer for Joe's Taco Lounge, Mill Valley

Fig-sized red and orange all-year Christmas bulbs
splash their holy light on the plastic-coated tablecloths
and glint against the bottled throats of every brand

of hot sauce — El Yucateco, Tapatio, Doña Maria's
Mole, singing their fiery songs on a shelf that lines the room,
nestled among a hundred ceramic Madonnas —

Tamazula, Cholula and Crystal beside the beatific
faces of the Mother of us all — and still lifes of hard
plastic fruit not invented in this country, not even

in the '40s, and so many crosses, empty and occupied,
paintings of Jesus and the Lord. O, Bufalo,
Valentina, Tabasco, Habañero, guard the bas-relief

bull's head glowering out of its red velvet frame, bless
the photograph of somebody's mother, and the bluefin
tuna leaping on the wall, river of traffic flowing

past the plate glass, sanctify each hot tortilla,
each yellow plastic basket lined with greasy paper,
watch over the customers tonight as they bend

their heads to quesadillas and burritos, Del Fuerte,
if you are listening, carry us safely into tomorrow,
we will praise you by the artificial light of every

electrified tabletop candle, O gods of the spoon-shaped,
the smooth-skinned, searing chiles, comfort us —
keep us warm.

Kindling

I watched you with those dry stone walls, the fitting and shifting,
using gravity, shape and no mortar, sweating, splitting the meaning

finer and finer, as if it were kindling. I learned about work
from following your obstinate tracks on the page.

My family gave me your general terrain: the late September aster,
brooks, birches, moon of standing water shining back at me

from ruts in the Dowsville Road. But you gave me the stated pain,
the thing said, found the smile inside your loneliness and wore it.

No one else cried Reluctance and Acceptance in the same breath,
or talked to smoke, cracked subtle jokes at God's expense.

How I loved your old clothes, woven of ambition and patience,
and the idea of Job's wife's disgust, backlit by her husband's earnestness.

My respect is partly inherited, although I doubt you'd recognize
my mother, the acolyte, so happy you had dipped one foot in the Pacific

that she cried, reluctant emigré to California, reading your poems aloud,
over and over, trying to herd all her children into sleep.

for Robert Frost

Kindness

Half-way through our nap the rain begins, hits the window,
plashes through the double-needled pines, and splurts down

onto the mule's ears and rein orchids, the clustered blue-faced
penstemons, sinking without a trace into the granite soil.

I roll gently out from under his arm and watch him sleeping the sleep
of the sunburned, of the good son, the wall-primer and painter,

the sleep of a man who is truly tired and knows someone
loves him, since I unaccountably began to cry about it over lunch

and couldn't stop, watching him eat was suddenly
too much for me, thinking how easily he could have died

in that fall, how he wandered lonely in the wilderness of his own mind,
never mind that people cared for him, for so long, twenty years,

long enough for me to get my second wind, to begin again
to grow up, so that I recognized true love when I saw it, looked

beyond the gnarled teeth and broken nose, the central, longitudinal scar
that runs his length from trachea to pubis, beyond the lost names

and repeated stories into kindness, so that when he began the steep
climb out of his brainpan's maze into stronger light, how lucky

I was there at the top of the stairs, passing by.

for Tad

First Winter

A cold night, the power out, and February,
where they are slowly chipping calico
layers of wallpaper off a kitchen ceiling,
balanced on wooden ladders they dragged
from under a tarp in the barn. Votives on the counter,
and in the next room their first necessary fire.
She has taught him to make quesadillas,
leave room for the milk in her tea.
He's taught her he won't leave.
Together, they have painted the living room
Black-Eyed Susan yellow, planted lilacs.
They don't know how hard it will be.
The first layer of paper's crisp black and red
is as painful, in the old house, as the place
where the scraper slices his palm. Blood
wells to match the ceiling, a few bright
drops splash, almost lost on the spattered
linoleum floor. She hunts up a band-aid,
abandoned in the medicine chest, and wipes the cut
clean with an old towel. They have made their vows.
Candlelight spins the shadows of their hands
across rain-slick window glass. They scrape
until their shoulders ache, through decades
of paper, past all their college blue books, diaphragms
and operettas, past the damp palms of high school dances,
the caught frogs and molding petri dishes of third grade,
to the smiles of their exhausted mothers
on the different days they were born,
each successive layer softer-toned and sweeter
than the last, until they reach gold roses
on pale green stems, and stop to admire them.

What to Wear

You stand in front of a mirror to ponder the question.
You look at yourself boldly, the way he would,
from all angles, as if your body were one idea, a new
philosophical age, not just a series of curved lines intersecting.
The age of pleasure. You lift a breast in your palm, flesh
softer than singing, the flaccid nipple gilded by sunlight
streaming in from the yard, and you are thinking of his hand
holding this weight, and your heart beneath it,
of what he agrees to carry. You will cover yourself with cloth,
a beaded necklace, and wait for the pleasure of taking them off
while he's watching, his eyes going dark and his breath
stopped, just for a second, in his throat, your nipples rising
to the touch of wide fingers, the way this one
has risen now at the thought, your skin awake again
because in this world it is always morning, and summer,
and you are somewhere near the ocean, you can hear its
beat on the sand, and you are thinking of pouring
your whole body into his open mouth, the sweet and salt together.

Poem for the Rest of Us

No, yours is not the kind of beauty that from afar stops men's breath.
But your hair falls copper beech leaves in September and honey
down your back, so heavy in a lover's hands he knows it as the gold
he's been seeking, twining it through his fingers, humming, and rain
runs in the gutters or the sun pours in a window or snow settles quietly
beside the pond—it doesn't matter. Yours is not the kind of beauty
that wilts in less than perfect weather, a hailstorm just brightens the gleam
in your eyes, the biting wind a more delicate woman might cringe from
gilds your face pink: you laugh at its stamina and dedication. No,
you don't have the sort of loveliness that men appreciate on museum walls—
Vermeer or Sargent blessing a swan-white neck, a luminous eye—
you can only be understood in motion: lifting a stack of dessert plates
to the top shelf, heaving jack-hammered rubble into the wheelbarrow's
ready maw and tossing a smile over your shoulder, cocking a hip
to stop the anticipated bang of a screen door. Your kind of beauty exists
close at hand. In the angle of wrist when you palm his chin and lean
in for the kiss. In the softness of lip against hungry lip.

Another Way of Asking

How can it be a coincidence that the woman
who as a child was given too much: forced, bent,
entered, and split open, and who therefore
learned to mute her own chords, to hide
the bright synaptic tunes of clavicle, instep and thigh,
would reach the balance point between yesterday
and what-happens-next and have to wet her lips
and beg for it, lying after the hundredth *I'm sorry*
in the restless shadows of anything,
Mannix, the Discovery Channel, salt on her cheek,
silver blade of a headache angling down
between her open eyes and a thin breeze failing
to lift the curtain? How can this not be God
laughing again?

Casual Sex

What is it I have not said —
       that your cock in my mouth
             leaves an imprint long after
                  I've forgotten your name —

That who I am exists intact
       whether you leave or stay — I
             haven't told you yet to go
                  but I'm afraid if you remain

here, settle in, I'll get so bored.
       I didn't mention your lower lip
             is beautiful because vulnerable,
                  or that nothing's the same

for hours after you leave my bed,
       headboard quivering, sheets aflame.

Color

Washington Square – New York, 1941

When Edward Hopper finishes his painting for the night,
sets the boar bristles to soak in turpentine, wipes the thick
not-yet-crusted-over drips from his smock with a blue rag
and tips his palette up to incubate tomorrow's luck,

he isn't thinking of the greenish light from a street lamp,
how it hits plate glass and fractures through it, or the counter's
corner in an all-night city diner. Most of the time
he is just hungry, already smelling the stew his wife

likes to make from white beans and bacon. His eyes lose focus,
and his other senses—so long ignored in deference
to saturated color—come alive, more vivid now
because of their confinement. How clear the little *click* as

the lamp's wick sinks below its silver mouth, scritch of boot heels
on the tile stair when he descends. He inhales the evening,
the butcher's bloody work, stale malt that drifts from a window.
The snowy world receives him: flakes melt and run down his cheeks.

The Color of Apricots

Someday, if you are lucky, your eyes will open
a little wider than usual and take it all in:
the Anna's hummingbird hovering in the bottlebrush
next to a Monarch, bougainvillea the color of apricots,
tiny blooms on the sharp-scented rosemary blue as the sky,
the green plates of nasturtium leaves angling after the sun,
and behind you a roar of salt water carrying all the higher notes
so you can't distinguish a buzzing fly from the chain saw
someone is using next door to trim a cypress
or the traffic copter over the bay.
It's almost Christmas. Glint of a plane overhead,
without sound. There is no religion here, no future.
Only the hot sun on your back and a one-eyed cat
ignoring the hummingbird. Soon the tide will come all the way in.
If you're lucky, you'll sit through the afternoon
in a splintered chair, elbows gracing a table whose planks
have weathered gray, and the ocean will pound the beach
as you listen, the chain saw sputter and finally die, the Monarch
touch at the edge of your glass and close his wings twice.

Missing him, suddenly

on the Interstate, one of those towns
where it's never not hot — the oleander bakes
between blistered lanes. It's not even summer.
At the crusted window I order a cheeseburger
and fries. I settle the paper sack in my lap,
partly in his honor, but also because
I am traveling: this is road food: at any hour,
accompanied by a styrofoam cup of weak iced tea
and maybe a cigarette, it can improve
your driving—this time of year when those little
anonymous carpets of roadside vegetation
begin to bloom, a two-week window
when their insistent yellow matches the center line
so exactly it's a miracle, a signal from God or
outer space or whatever we still believe in.

Tiles on a Temple Wall at Luanphrabang

Chipped, loosening history's clenched jaws,
    pasted along the outer walls
        under a wooden gutter

delicate blue-glass armies of Lao
    fight with curved swords,
        the heads of their enemies lopped off
            and scattered on the ground.

Thai and Chinese millions fall, glittering
    where the sun misses banana-leaf shade,
        a dinner-plate hibiscus,
            and strikes the temple corner.

Water buffalo and square-wheeled wagons roll
    down brown lanes, grain is baled
        in sheaves of gold bound by green-glass cord.

Ladies dance in black-glass dresses, elbows high,
    wrists cocked impossibly back,
        near breaking.

Sunlight on the Mekong reflects up two hundred stairs,
    illuminates a pair of grey-glass elephants
        and riding on their backs:
            the long-dead king and queen.

The October Garden

If you were zinnia, still bright
in the October garden and I the last
orange cosmos. If you were catmint blue
draping yourself over the cinder block wall
and I the weed coming up through gravel.
If you were the bamboo pole, listing
under the weight of late green tomatoes
that will never ripen now, and I
the frayed string that binds them. If
you were heavy purple grapes dangling
over the canted railing and I the feasting
thrush. If you were summer's echo
in yellow coreopsis and I the tall sedum,
autumn-flushed. If you were the sun
breaking slant over that little grove of aspens
across the street, if you were hummingbird's
quick wing, if you were winter coming on
or the studious worm and I the turned
earth, the patch of moss beneath an oak,
the oak's sharp-edged leaf ready to crackle
underfoot, the white-throated sparrow's
familiar three descending notes in a minor
key, oh, if only I were sometimes
you and you were me.

Anger

Pantoum Without Hope of Rescue

This time it's both of them,
half-clothed on their own double bed,
mother and father, husband and wife.
If this upsets you, by all means turn away.

Half-clothed on their own double bed,
their daughter naked between them.
If this upsets you, by all means turn away:
look at the expensive view of the Golden Gate.

Their daughter, naked between them,
used to being invisible flesh.
Look at the expensive view of the Golden Gate.
Think about justice as an abstraction.

Used to being invisible flesh,
she lies with her shoulders in her mother's lap.
Think about justice as an abstraction —
perhaps you'll never need a witness yourself.

She lies with her shoulders in her mother's lap.
They run their hands across her skin like feathers.
Perhaps you'll never need a witness yourself.
The father pushing his way into her.

They run their hands across her skin like feathers.
He likes to hold her legs up as if it's a game,
her father, pushing his way into her,
grinning and panting, saying how good it will feel.

He likes to hold her legs up as if it's a game,
leaning over the child to kiss his happy wife,
grinning and panting, saying how good it will feel,
palming her breasts, glazed with fine sweat.

Leaning over the child to kiss his happy wife
as if they were alone there,
palming her breasts, glazed with fine sweat.
No one is angry. No one cries.

As if they were alone there,
mother and father, husband and wife.
No one is angry. No one cries,
although this time, it's both of them.

Deconstruction

In the end, we never had the conversation:
  where were you when he..., and—
    how could you not have noticed?

She never said —
  I'm so sorry you were harmed, I'd give my left arm to have saved you.
Instead,
  well, you know how he was, no one could stop him.
This must be how I learned, at ten or twelve, to carry my life
  in my own hands, to walk steadily toward anyone's rage,
    not flinching.

As she lies on the hospital bed I can see myself in her drawn face,
  the cheekbones, angle of nostrils, and he
    inhabits my wrists and eyes and shoulders.
But I am not really their daughter, after all.

I am the child of narcissism and panic, of cause and its friend effect,
  and any resemblance to them is purely coincidence.

Daughters

I am looking over my grandfather's plaid shoulder
examining the molding of a door frame
inch by creamy white inch. The door
is ajar—he forgot to close it
all the way when he came in.

I am using a trick my father taught me:
to get through bouts of nausea on long car trips
he told me to watch the horizon.
I used that technique when he came for me, later
latching my eyes to a spot out the window—
sometimes the Alcatraz light— and tried to block
sensation out: smell of his skin, deep voice
humming, the thump of his body against me.

Two-thirds of a face appears in the door, brown hair
curls around it, summer green dress, no shoes.
I am looking directly at my mother.
Grandpa's pipe hand is over my mouth, I gag
on the smell of Holiday tobacco.
The whispering noise of his corduroy pants
against the chair is only birch trees
in the wind. She is frozen, lips
half-drawn back, as if about to speak.
Her eyes are glazed, not looking
into mine. She turns her head slowly
the way an old dog will, stupid with sleep,
and walks out of the frame.

Defenses Against Unbearable Sorrow

When you can't think of anything else to write, you can still go down to the
beach and scratch your name in the sand.

If you aren't near the ocean, write in the dirt, or pour sugar on the counter.
If you don't have a name, use mine.

If there's no paper, write on your napkin, or the underside of
a loquat leaf stolen
from somebody's yard.
Try the pitted, scented rind of a lemon.
You can pull brown paper sacks out of dumpsters, use doubled leaves of that
flimsy toilet paper from public restrooms.
Write anything.
Scrawl whatever you have to say on the side wall of the Shell station, or across
the placid face of the 2AM Club's red front doors.

When you don't have a pen or a pencil you can cut the
edge of your palm with a
knife, or a piece of broken glass from the street,
and write with blood.

Or, if you're still young enough, and a woman, you can slide a finger
up into your vagina for some menstrual blood.

It's darker than anything else on the page.

Light

Theology

A leftover moon in the hour
before the hour before sunrise
silvers the deck's planks, an empty
flower pot's rim, throws a crazy
shadow of branches from a bare
maple across the asphalt road.
It's easy to understand why
this is the season they needed
God, had to invent him or die
of loneliness, the world barren,
colder and darker every day,
nothing in that terrifying
interval between their bowed heads
and the glint of wheeling stars.

Winter Sun

How valuable it is in these short days,
threading through empty maple branches,
the lacy-needled sugar pines.

Its glint off sheets of ice tells the story
of Death's brightness, her bitter cold.

We can make do with so little, just the hint
of warmth, the slanted light.

The way we stand there, soaking in it,
mittened fingers reaching.

And how carefully we gather what we can
to offer later, in darkness, one body to another.

Double Solitaire

We have started to play double solitaire,
he to practice flexing his brain, I to learn more
patience, and this morning, when he gets up at four,
flicks the light so he can find his work clothes
and begins to talk to me about nothing, I wake too,
first grudgingly, annoyed, and then completely,
putting my patience to the test, excited by the dark.

While he has a cigarette I brush my teeth, avoiding
the beetle trapped in the copper sink, not drowning it
with toothpaste but still too groggy for any kind of rescue.
The rest of the house — sisters and nephews and brothers-
in-law, two cats, a dog, a goldfish, the uncountable
winged creatures — is asleep. We shuffle the cards
as quietly as we know how, place them on the table

seven across without the flip and snap we're used to.
Each of us has our own game, but we share the aces.
The decks are slipperier than the ones we use at home
and a jack of clubs slides into my lap. It looks
so much like him, uncrowned, that my throat closes.
I want to know what it's like to lose your mind
as he did, and remake it, over decades,

playing solitaire with the woman who loves you
instead of high-stakes poker, the straight roads inside your head
turning into mountain lanes, switching back on each other,
suddenly one-way. How many dead ends does he run into
every day and what does it take to back up, turn around
and try to get where he's going? He remembers my name, but not
how to make a blank page come up in his computer, not

the name of his new boss, unless I say "Robert E." and then
he finishes "Lee." I don't know what to do except deal out the cards,
not rushing to put my three on his two of hearts but not holding back
too long either—it's not in my nature, and it would be condescending.
I just watch him in his measured way unfold his hand and play
what he's been dealt, black five on the red six, jack on the queen,
a quartered peach and two cups of coffee steaming in white cups
between us.

In the Fifth Year of Our War

Old swimming pool bending afternoon light
into turquoise, the water blown a little
by a circling wind, the usual summer chaff —
pine needles and leaves, pollen — eddying
across its glass surface. And a few drowned
wasps, their paper wings spread wide
as the wings of angels.

Behind the pool and out of sight, a creek
in full September growl creates a liquid
dissonance, the sound unfathomable.
A blue oak's high canopy floats over this
little dell, this haven, this American back yard,
softening its edges with rippling shade.
A place of easy generosity, offering itself
without bitterness or regret to anyone.

It's All Poetic

in the end, the low hum of insects
dismantling a body, buzz and tug,
the skin's flakes disappearing
into tiny mandibles, the eggs laid
in too-soft, soon-to-be-putrid flesh.
There's a loveliness to every ruined
thing—the chassis accordioned
beside Highway 20 gleams in noon light
like a wished-on penny. Shit sinks
through the tank's dark layers
with slow grace, giving up its liquid
to green the world overhead. Show me
something with no beauty. You can't.
The father entering his own child?
Beyond the tears, see how their closed
eyes are exactly the same shape.

What I Want

is to inhabit
the world as it is:

the crab apple's
magenta halo

shading a squirrel
crushed into the road —

me not turning
my eyes away.

Full Dark

Tonight, inside my body, the blood races through veins,
passing in its circuit a piece of chicken wire. Calling it something
homely gives me all the power over the stent I'm ever going to have:
thus does woman return to Eden and name the world. But tonight,
I'm not a woman, just a body whose heart's still beating.
I could be elk, frog, house cat, spawning salmon. A raptor
sailing above its next morsel. I could be the morsel.
My friend whose chest was cracked years ago is still astonished
that you can't feel anything with your heart. There's no sensation,
only the blind clenching and unclenching, a machine.
I'll tell you what scares me most: how fast it beats.
Tonight, the last birds scatter goodbyes across the lawn.
The sky's that nearly sherbet color I can't match with paint.
Life is full of minor disappointments. Failures of skill, failures of wit,
of luck. That the heart can't feel a thing is pretty funny—
love being only in our minds, after all. Tonight, the light will drain
from air the way it always does and then the blue hour descend
and then full dark. I'm still as brave as I was before the careful
insertion of chicken wire: not more, not less. Probably,
like my father, and his father—with or without salt, soy, egg yolks,
butter, exercise, and wonder—I will live as long as I live.
Not a moment longer.

Time

Because the Past Is Just Another Neighborhood

Isn't it something, when you can reach back 30 years for a photograph—
go right to it in the album—glue long-evaporated—lift it from
the yellowed sleeve, hold the faded color between your thumb and forefinger,
photograph your brother took the week you left for college: rounded back end
of your half-ton Chevy, '53, whose linkage stuck downshifting into first
every third or fourth light so you had to get out and pop the hood,
rattle that gear some guy showed you could be rattled, and then, to a chorus
of horns, in your hiking boots and long green calico skirt from MGM's
costume sale on Divisadero, hop back in and, burning a little rubber,
waving *sorry!* to the line of cars behind you, twist the radio up
for "Teach Your Children."

I Think of Them

going a little gray, the skin beginning to loosen over their muscles.
How they held my face in their various hands, the names they gave me.

The one with too much money—shoulders wide as Ohio—who wanted
to be a scallop-diver. Another who fell asleep mid-sentence at dinner.
The house painter who went to chamber concerts by himself.

Their shoes on the stairs, neatly twinned or tossed in passing,
laces tangled. Their surfboards and tennis rackets stacked in the garage,
half-empty tubes of ski-wax.

                              Sometimes their fingers still play in my hair.
I hold them when they're drunk, when the Red Sox lose, the car dies—
when their cocks unaccountably won't unfurl.

I take our old arguments back over the same ground and I leave again
for all the same reasons.

I think of the children they had later, without me.
I think of them at night or in the morning when I'm driving
and some stupid song comes on—the one we kissed to, breathing it sweet
into each others' mouths, back when we had all the time in the world.

How to Be Lonely

When your friends take you to the county fair,
be grateful. Cook three-course dinners for one.
Walk in the hills only on moonless nights.
Leave the phone in its cradle. Always come home
to a darkened house. Dwell on what it was like
to be touched. Think of him with the next lover.
Imagine the aftermath of a nuclear war
and you alive, alone, unharmed on an ashy plain.
Appreciate the more difficult beauty:
underside of the leaf, back of the fabric.

Belonging

Long after I'd remembered most of it, after
my mother had said, "You've wrecked my life,"
and Ellen asked me not to send her the poems
because they ruined her sex life, and Tom
wondered aloud if I was recalling a past life,
after Nan said over the phone, "By the way,
I don't believe you," and Henry told
some of my friends at dinner
that I'd always been a liar,
after I'd gained a hundred pounds
and begun to carry it like an open window,
and after enough time had passed
to dull my anger down to a simmer
I walked to the kitchen one day—
a sunny day, a Tuesday—
heading for Håagen Dazs or Ben & Jerry's
and caught my face in the mirror unawares:
the rosy cheeks, slight clench in the jaw
and looked back at myself, directly,
with my father's eyes, the purpose in them clear,
all the power he carried toward my bed
that I was bearing in the direction of ice cream
and I understood how humans
do what they do, how they can't not do it,
and at that moment I loved my father,
so dangerous and helpless,
and loved myself for loving him again.

Not Nantucket

From one day to the next, I forget how inexorably the light rises
beyond the hill beyond my house — Cement Hill, named
by frustrated miners in 1850 — how when I'm facing west,
the pines are lit from the top, needle by needle and branch
by lifted branch. Light ratchets down their silhouettes, then
telephone poles and then the willows — even the knots
of blackberry vines illumined, limned and shining. Yes, like a blessing.

Today the sun on its rounds speaks to me only of time
going too fast, of summer's ending, of how many Augusts I might
have left. If I live as long as my father, I'll have three — it's a kind
of blasphemy, isn't it? To outlast our parents? Not dying after they die,
but getting more years than they were given. A type of disloyalty.
Yet I hope to be disloyal. How closely we're tied to our gene pool,
to the breakfasts we ate as kids, to Martha's Vineyard

and not Nantucket. We're made specifically in their image —
the Mother and Father gods — with nature v. nurture thrown in
for good measure and how many of us not walking the path
our parents trod are treading its opposite? Exactitude in rebellion
is no less exact. We're so helpless to be different from the way we are.
The older I get, the grayer, the more my hair curls itself into a picture
of my mother — hair that was never her color or weight when I was younger.

From malleable stuff we solidify into the family model: smart, dumb,
easy-to-please or unforgiving. Good at adding the tip to a restaurant tab
and dividing by seven diners, one who didn't have wine. Able to make
those fish-scale tracks uphill on cross-country skis — or not. Very rarely,
and only when the stakes are high, can we throw off the mantle.
As when laying a finger against the downy cheek of a sleeping child,
we know to go no further. We stop.

Travel

Even though you've been here before,
it's as new as his right hand uncurling from the gear shift
and hunting for yours while he keeps his eyes on the curved road,
although you weren't crying loudly enough for him to hear,
hadn't even started to follow the thought, only an image
of your father's face receding in the side view mirror — mirage
or nightmare, it doesn't matter — tears coming on of their own accord
and the radio spitting a little between syllables of Tom Petty's drawl.
You tell him you love him, but despite all the big talk
you're still afraid to be known. Pine trees wheeling
past the windshield tower over you as surely as a parent
looms above his own child, the one he invented.
It's early or late, and the wind is picking up. This is as new
as the look in his eyes when he says he loves you and isn't kidding
or trying to get you to make dinner. Wherever you are going,
it is winter and summer, it is midnight. You are almost there.

Love Songs

Many miles into nowhere, a light snow falling,
softening fence rails and telephone lines—no wind.

Beyond the wipers and the slish of tires on asphalt:
a palpable quiet. It's a night for not driving

toward anything or away, closing in on home with gas
to get there and somebody crooning from the radio. Love songs.

It's getting late. The singer is old now, tapping his foot
against a wheelchair's silver rim in half-remembered rhythm,

parked in the hall of a nursing home, trumpet and bass
and the rest disbanded, instruments dumb in their cases

but still we can hear them, a long time ago when they were young,
the glad notes lifting. A little static rising now from the radio

interrupts them. Snow still falling. Grey pelt of raccoon
curled by the roadside under his thin shroud and above him

Soft Shoulder, the yellow highway diamond's benediction.
This is how it will happen. When the wheels have slowed

and rolled to a stop and the sky filled with its final white.
When the maps are folded back into careful rectangles.

When all the crows are silent, the glasses emptied of wine,
cigarettes stubbed out in the tin ashtrays

of motel rooms. When the last string of a guitar is plucked
and one last song's hushed note drifts above us,

all that's left weightless and eloquent, disappearing like smoke.

for Dorianne

Notes to the Poems

p. 34 "Rowing, November" refers to the Charles River in Cambridge, MA.

p. 35 *Ha Ha Ha* translates to 555 in Lao, which is a British brand of cigarette manufactured in Laos before the Viet Nam war. Its factory in the capital city of Vientiane was made into a hotel in 1988.

p. 36 Doe Bay is on Orcas Island, one of Washington State's San Juan Islands.

p. 37 "Not All Who Wander Are Lost" was written for Tom Taylor.

p. 45 The song is "Weel May the Keel Row," an anonymous folk song first printed in Edinburgh, 1770 (*The Penguin Book of English Folk Songs,* 112).

p. 54 "Poem for the Rest of Us" was inspired by a line from Julia Kelliher.

p. 60 "The Color of Apricots" was written for Carol.

p. 62 Luangphrabang is the old capital city of Laos and houses the royal palace.

p. 85 The Chevy truck is long gone, but can be seen on the cover of "Using Your Turn Signal Promotes World Peace." (Photo credit, Peter Fisk.) Divisadero St. is in San Francisco. Graham Nash wrote "Teach Your Children"— it's on the 1970 Crosby, Stills, Nash, and Young album, *Déjà Vu,* with Jerry Garcia playing pedal steel (in exchange for harmony lessons for the Dead).

p. 88 The people's names in "Belonging" have been changed. The ice cream brands have not.

Molly Fisk teaches poetry privately and runs the popular on-line workshop Poetry Boot Camp (poetrybootcamp.com). She teaches cancer patients and caregivers to boost their immune systems through writing. Molly speaks on the subjects of creativity, power, and child abuse. Her fellowship and grant awards in Poetry include the National Endowment for the Arts, the California Arts Council, and the Marin (County, CA) Arts Council, and her poetry has been awarded the Dogwood Prize, Robinson Jeffers Tor House Prize, Billee Murray Denny Prize, and the National Writers' Union Prize. She lives in the Sierra foothills in California.

Breinigsville, PA USA
01 March 2010
233319BV00001B/1/P